MW01109361

199 ideas

Member Service and Engagement

PUBLISHED BY
ASAE: THE CENTER FOR ASSOCIATION LEADERSHIP

The Center for Association Leadership

WASHINGTON, DC

The contributors have worked diligently to ensure that all information in this book is accurate as of the time of publication and consistent with standards of good practice in the general management community. As research and practice advance, however, standards may change. For this reason it is recommended that readers evaluate the applicability of any recommendations in light of particular situations and changing standards.

ASAE: The Center for Association Leadership
1575 I Street, NW
Washington, DC 20005-1103
Phone: (202) 626-2723; (888) 950-2723 outside the metropolitan Washington, DC area
Fax: (202) 220-6439
Email: books@asaecenter.org
We connect great ideas and great people to inspire leadership and achievement in the association community.

Keith C. Skillman, CAE, Vice President, Publications, ASAE: The Center for Association Leadership
Baron Williams, CAE, Director of Book Publishing, ASAE: The Center for Association Leadership

Cover design by Beth Lower, Art Director, ASAE: The Center for Association Leadership and Troy Scott Parker, Cimarron Design
Interior design by Troy Scott Parker, Cimarron Design

This book is available at a special discount when ordered in bulk quantities. For information, contact the ASAE Member Service Center at (202) 371-0940.

A complete catalog of titles is available on the ASAE: The Center for Association Leadership website at www.asaecenter.org.

ISBN-13: 978-0-88034-327-5
ISBN-10: 0-88034-327-3

Copyright © 2011 by ASAE: The Center for Association Leadership.

All rights reserved. Permission to reproduce or transmit in any form or by any means, electronic or mechanical, including photocopying and recording, or by an information storage and retrieval system any portion of this work must be obtained in writing from the director of book publishing at the address or fax number above.

Printed in the United States of America.

10 9 8 7 6 5 4 3 2 1

CONTENTS

Introduction and Acknowledgments v

Member Service 1

Frontline Member Service 1

Member-centric Mindset 7

Communication Techniques 10

What Not to Say 17

Education 17

Back Office Customer Service 20

Components 24

Marketing 25

Engagement 31

Welcoming New Members 32

Engaging Members Through Benefits and Services 35

Preparing Members for the Future 35

Keep Them Coming Back 37

Leveraging Your Website and Social Media 38

Engaging Members Through Relationships 42

See It Through Their Eyes 42

Create a Collaborative Environment 44

Make Member Connections 45

Communicate 45

Moving Members from Engaged to Involved 48

Volunteer Recognition 48

Volunteer Opportunities 49

Share Tips with Colleagues 53

INTRODUCTION AND ACKNOWLEDGMENTS

In 2009 we published the first of our "199 Ideas" series booklets: *199 Ideas: Membership Recruitment and Retention.* Consider this the logical extension of the ideas expressed in that first volume—the books go hand in hand, addressing areas of concern that are at the very tops of the lists of all who work in membership organizations. We're really all about engagement. We know that from experience. We know that from research findings expressed in both ASAE's *The Decision to Join* (2007) and *The Decision to Volunteer* (2008): Member loyalty goes up exponentially with level of involvement.

This booklet views engagement broadly and comprises two parts. The first offers tested ideas for delivering exceptional member service, underscoring the principle that success in the realm of membership retention hinges to a great degree on the service and treatment of members. The second part focuses on ways to engage members in meaningful activity that will bind them to your organization—a key thread of the engagement section is that of moving members from affiliation to engagement to involvement.

Many but not all of the ideas here will apply or be adaptable to your organization. While there is no one-size-fits-all set of solutions, we hope that each of the tips in this book will drive home a fundamental, freshen up an old standard, or spark your imagination in ways that help your organization better serve and engage its membership.

The ideas here were culled, adapted, and compiled from many years of stories told in ASAE: The Center for Association Leadership publications and from tips generously contributed by colleagues like you. If you find something here that you can use, please consider giving back to the community by sharing a tip for possible inclusion in future publications. Check out the back pages of this book or go to **www.asaecenter.org/sharemytip**. Our "199 Ideas" series is always growing, and we're always looking for ideas in many topic areas.

Our sincerest thanks to the following contributors and to all those who share their experiences through ASAE: The Center for Association Leadership:

EXECUTIVE EDITOR

Caryl Tynan
American College of Phlebology

CONTRIBUTING EDITORS

Tip Tucker Kendall
Women's Basketball Coaches Association

Linda Brady
Association for Healthcare Documentation Integrity

CONTRIBUTORS

Tony Rossell
Marketing General, Inc.

Cynthia Simpson
Association for Women in Science

Katherine Swartz
Columbia Opportunity Resource

Linda Chreno

Celena Nuquay
NAFSA: Association of International Educators

Kevin Whorton
Whorton Marketing & Research

Caroline Fuchs

Bruce Sanders
American College of Phlebology

Don Dea
Fusion Productions

Amy Lestition
Association Media and Publishing (formerly SNAP)

Stuart Meyer
Social Frequency Media Communications

Miriam Miller
United Fresh Produce Association

Dana Deponzi-Haas
American College of Phlebology

Scott Oser
Scott Oser Associates

MEMBER SERVICE

1. Member service is everyone's mission.

This does not mean that your authority in this area need be diminished, but it is vitally important that everyone live the marketing policies developed by you and your association. If total excellence is part of your marketing thrust, then everyone from the CEO to the data entry clerk should actively demonstrate those principles and continually seek ways in which to incorporate those principles into their daily work. Everyone in your organization is responsible for member service; whether or not your employees have a direct link with the member, they all have an effect on member service. Engaging members should be the job of every staff person. When the opportunity arises, each staffer needs to make the member experience as satisfying as possible.

2. Why you should bend over backwards for your members.

Members will generally develop an impression of you for one of two reasons: Your products or services are particularly poor, or your products or services are extremely good. Which impression are you leaving? The worst impression? To leave no impression at all because your products, benefits and member service reps are so lackluster. If member service is impeccable, there will be less emphasis on what you can't do for them. Engaging members properly requires listening and providing what is needed and at the least leaving them with a clear answer and the feeling that someone has taken the time to listen and react, even when the answer may not be exactly what was needed.

3. Even if there is no competition for your business, your members deserve the best service.

If there were no Honda or Ford or Dodge, does that mean General Motors customers deserve to be treated like nobodies, or worse, treated well only because GM is afraid someone's going to start another car company and steal them? Of course not.

4. Eliminate opportunities to fail.

If you remove all of the avenues through which members can become dissatisfied, members will stay. Then you can invest your time in absolutely delighting them. The theoretical goal is not to live from dues payment to dues payment; it's to have enough extra money in the member bank to splurge all the time.

5. Moderate authority.

Give your staff responsibility for members' satisfaction. Knowing that their treatment of members is what will make the association thrive—or fail—is very inspirational. Empower reps to handle transactions (within limits, of course) so that members don't have to be put on hold, or worse, called back. Members resent waiting for a rep having to go ask a supervisor for the answer to a question; they could have just called the supervisor to begin with, right?

6. A voice.

Member service reps are in the trenches every day; who knows better what members are saying, good, bad, or otherwise? Try leaving time at least every week for comments. Set up a suggestion box for staff and members to vicariously express concerns. Ignoring valid comments from reps and/or members can do serious damage to your retention rate. Be sure to acknowledge the comments—even if they cannot be acted upon.

7. Knowledge that allows reps to think on their feet.

Your employees must be able to explain the "who-what-when-where-how-and-why" to members. Develop and keep up-to-date a listing of FAQs. One of the best ways to arm reps for member questions—of any kind—is to role-play with your FAQ list (see the Checklist on page TBD for an example; it's a good idea to compile a list of questions members ask most often and come up with a standard set of answers). Have reps take turns asking each other these questions plus a few really tough ones (everyone will have a few to bring to the discussion, believe me). Do this exercise in "flash card" fashion until everyone knows the answers down pat. Now throw a few curve balls; if reps whiff it, it's because they don't have a good enough grasp of the underlying reasons for the answers they provided to the flash card questions. Back to the training board. Ask the reps to develop a listing of their most common and most unusual questions to help further expand the FAQ list.

8. Fair warning.

When there's anything new to introduce or something's about to change, please don't let the reps be the last to know. For example, when you're about to launch a mailing campaign, please give samples of the pieces you're mailing (and mailing dates) to the reps so they know what members are referring to when they call. Don't blindside your reps; it makes them feel like they're completely out of the loop and diminishes the "team." In fact, everyone should receive a copy of messages that you are sending out. If they are talking to a member about a communication from headquarters and don't know anything about it, it doesn't look good!

9. Review often.

Know your stuff! Open that manual once in a while and re-read a little at a time. Do a pop quiz at a service team meeting and give a prize for the most correct answers (Starbucks coffee gift card, an extra hour for lunch, etc.) If you're really on top of your job, you'll spend less time interrupting other reps and keeping members on hold while you try to get the information.

10. Try a job-for-a-day program.

An Idaho CEO almost completely redesigned his management structure based on time he spent doing six different membership jobs; retention was up 12 percent the following year. Anyone and everyone can be trained to take inquiries, process applications, handle mailings, develop retention concepts, and do exit interviews. This develops member empathy; it also provides coverage during staff absences.

11. Develop a "what else?" mentality.

Whenever a member requests anything—help, information, support, a product, a conference brochure—train your brain to think of something else you can "pile on" to make the member feel like he or she is getting an unexpected yet very pleasant surprise. Put yourself in your member's shoes on a frequent basis. If a member calls with a reference question, tell him or her you'll keep a tickler card in your file in case any additional information pertaining to the subject should come across your desk. That kind of treatment really makes people feel special.

12. Deliver beyond the standard.

If a member calls with a question you may have answered very adequately, take a few minutes to do some extra digging and see if you can offer a better answer. For example, if a member calls you wanting to know if your discount rental car benefit would be applicable for an overseas trip, verify that it is, then get on the web, find a list of recommended restaurants for the city to which he was traveling, and email it to the member. He or she will be floored. What would be the little extra you would like to receive when you call in?

13. Remove the intimidation factor.

If you're a rep for a very large association, new members may be somewhat overwhelmed by your range of benefits and available information. If you can, whittle down the main benefits and services, connect a name and telephone number/extension to each, print them on a little "How do I…?" internal phone directory card and include it in your new member packet. A Midwest association did this and increased the use of the library by nearly 20 percent among those in their first year of membership. Be sure to rotate the benefits described—and if something is updated or expanded, be sure to include that as well.

14. Perform a next-day checkup.

If a member calls with a particularly perplexing or difficult problem, take a moment to play "doctor" and do a follow-up visit. Call back the following day to see how everything's going and see that the "patient's" problem is satisfactorily resolved. It's an excellent opportunity to tie up any loose ends and ingratiate that member to your association for life. Use a tickler file for these reminders.

15. A real test.

Each week, take the time to call a member whom you know has not been pleased with your service in the past. Ask if there's anything the member needs, or if there's anything special you can do. Tell the member you're very interested in his or her satisfaction and are there to serve in whatever way is needed. An extraordinary effort, indeed, but one that will win the heart of even the crankiest member. Remember, the crankiness comes from something *you* did; look at it as your personal challenge to "uncrank" that member. Your maturity will be revered.

16. Train front-line employees.

Because member complaints are best resolved at the point of service, staff members need special training to handle specific situations—both those in which a solution can be found and those when it can't. Staff members must recognize when a problem exists.

The American Immigration Lawyers Association made customer service a priority with its Customer Service Initiative (originally called the "Front Liners Team"), an effort designed to improve customer service and educate all staff members. The team initially comprised everyone considered to be the front line of duty in dealing with customers, but later evolved to include everyone on staff. At each team meeting, staff members share examples of good or bad customer service that they've experienced. Someone gets a prize for who can be the funniest, or the worst, or the best. The goal is to take away something small from each session that the organization will implement and roll over into the culture. Eventually, the small changes will start to add up.

Adapted from: White, Aria. "Make Customer Service a Team Effort." *Associations Now,* November 2010, p. 16.

17. Welcome complaints.

When a member calls and starts complaining, thank him or her. Thanking a member for a complaint creates a feeling that you and the member are now in partnership against a common enemy. If you don't empathize, the member is going to link you with the problem, and then the member will have two enemies. You want to create a triangle that's composed of you and the member against the problem, not you and the problem against the member. It's also great to say things like, "Thank you for giving us an opportunity to improve," and "It's so helpful to know about things like this; we only have the power to fix problems if we know about them."

18. "If I ever have a problem, please help me with it."

Aside from benefits, this is a primary member "want." Complaints are inevitable, no matter how flawless your systems and staff might be. The way you handle your *faux pas* may determine whether a member renews. Focus on a solution for the customer first and work on repairing the cause after the customer has been helped.

19. What if your service reputation has suffered some damage?

Many associations don't realize that they can actually capitalize on the opportunity service recovery creates for strengthening member ties; if you come right out and say, "We haven't been very good at this, and here's our new plan for making things better," you'll get members' attention, and maybe even a little sympathy. A good service recovery program is easy to establish.

20. Initiate a performance watch.

Create tracking mechanisms that enable front-line employees to notify management almost immediately of problems that occur in their area; a daily "problem" log, kept by each rep, is a fast and effective way for managers to spot troublesome trends. This ad hoc system should complement regular member surveys.

21. Believe in your association!

If you believe in your association and what it represents chances are you are more likely to speak with conviction when conveying the importance of engagement or involvement to your members. Chances are your members will recognize this and continue to believe as well. Be sure to reinforce this to your active members and encourage them to provide testimonials or testify on behalf of your organization to their peers and other members.

22. Think like your members.

You're more likely to perform effectively if you if you keep their problems, needs, and viewpoints in mind. Projecting your own opinions onto members and assuming what they want often precludes you from meeting their needs. You can find out what your members really want and if you're providing value to them with the use of a variety of survey tools, such as focus groups, all-member surveys and new-member surveys.

23. This way out.

There are many, many more associations than there were ten years ago, and members often have a choice to go elsewhere if you're not treating them the way they want to be treated. People are also much less tolerant of poor service than they used to be, so you have to try harder and harder to keep them from leaving. Don't hold the door open for them by skimping on member service.

24. Make a mental shift.

When you think about it, we all provide services to others, every day. We willingly do things for our families, friends, and even strangers. So it seems that providing members with good service should come naturally to us. For most of us, it does not; somehow, we shift our focus when we enter work. Why? Because it's *required*. When you do something for a friend, the motivation is different; you do it because you want to, not because you're being paid to. Tomorrow, start thinking of your job as a helping profession rather than a service profession. Your behavior will undergo a marvelous transformation.

25. A member is the most important person in any association.
They equate to shareholders in a for-profit company. They own the association. If you need further convincing, think of it in terms of your paycheck. Who do you think is funding your paycheck when dues and non-dues revenue purchases made by members account for the vast majority of overall revenue for most associations?

26. A member call isn't an interruption of my work; it is the purpose of it.
Review the previous tip and remember that a member can sense your mood during a phone call. If deadlines are approaching and things are hectic when your phone rings, take a second to catch a deep breath, smile, then answer the phone to see how you can help.

27. Be a better empathizer.
In the most basic sense, this means putting yourself in another's shoes, but it's really more than that. When a member calls and says, "I'm about to lose my license because of a recordkeeping error," your reactions should ideally evolve like this:

1. It's awful that she might lose her license. She worked long and hard to achieve that, and it would be a great loss.

2. There appears to be an injustice here. She did not put herself in jeopardy; someone else's mistake did.

3. She needs legal help.

4. I know exactly how to help her. (Of course, you're presuming she's telling you the truth.)

If you express these emotions, the member will immediately feel like you've personally erected a safety net beneath her. It is impossible to underestimate the value of such an interaction. It is then critical that you follow through, all the while empathizing with her anxiety over getting this resolved as quickly as possible!

28. If there is any doubt in your mind, always rule in favor of the member.

He or she might be wrong, might not have all the facts, or perceive things differently. Remember, however, perception is 100 percent reality to the individual. That individual is also a member of your association, and if you don't rule in his or her favor, will probably be just the type to go packing. Unless the member is a real sticky-wicket and you want him gone anyway, always *try*.

29. Is member dissatisfaction ever acceptable?

Consider that every dissatisfied member "infects" ten more. In that case, a goal of 100 person satisfaction isn't too high. It may not be entirely realistic, but logic defies shooting for anything less.

30. A very hard truth.

Members are self-centered. Completely. They do not care about you, at least not until they get to know you personally. They have only shown up to see what you can do for them; the sooner you under-stand that and start doing for them, the better your retention rate will be.

31. Perception is reality.

If a member continually gets a voicemail greeting when he or she calls with a question, the member is going to perceive that you're aloof, unavailable, and uninterested in helping him or her. That's his or her reality, even though your reality is that you're just busy. When you're in the service business, *your* reality doesn't matter.

32. Words to work by.

Many members will not return bad service with bad behavior; *they will simply go away.*

33. A key quality.

The next time you do an interview for a member service rep, ask the applicant if he or she has done any volunteer work. It's an excellent indication of a genuine willingness to "serve."

34. Create a culture in your organization that every person is a membership representative.

Every person is responsible for retaining members. Empower your staff, in and out of your department, to help members. Use FAQ sheets, EZ links, and a list of contacts for specific programs or subjects.

35. When considering members, you should also consider nonmembers.

Nonmembers can provide a source of revenue as well. As they continually use your services, you should be regularly reminding them of the benefits of membership, and in time, they will see that the benefit outweighs the cost. If they don't benefit, then that is okay; they can still provide a revenue source.

36. When drafting messages, flyers, brochures and forms, think of your audience and what their point of view is.

Are your messages showing the value of membership? Are your flyers and brochures easy to read? Are your forms and processes easy to understand?

A great tagline can be the easiest, and most effective way to grab readers' attention and communicate your association's impact or promote one of your programs or special events. To write a terrific tagline: research, review and test for effectiveness. Make sure you love your tagline and will be satisfied using it for years to come. However, down the road a tagline change can freshen your message and rejuvenate your association's brand.

Adapted from: Schwartz, Nancy E. "10 Terrific Taglines, and 9 Traps to Avoid." *Communication News*, December 2010.

Communication Techniques

37. Keep your word.

If a service rep doesn't do what he or she promises, how can you call it service? It's human nature for people to want to please other people, so they'll say things in the moment, but fail to deliver later on. Learn how to watch your words, and make sure that everything you say can be backed up with action.

38. He (or she) who answers member/customer emails or phone calls provides a lasting impression of the organization.

For almost all associations, the "primary company contact" is the person who answers general emails and the phone. Lack of a prompt response conveys understaffing and disorganization— callers will make all kinds of assumptions. The impression made through email or phone responses can even make or break a decision to engage with the organization.

39. Respond quickly.

Set expectations for individuals who email or phone so they know, as quickly as possible, when to expect a response to their inquiry. A timely acknowledgement of the inquiry with an estimated time for the complete response, and a contact name, will go a long way towards building rapport and demonstrating credibility.

40. Create a set of frequently asked questions.

When a member contacts the organization, they're on a mission— especially if they need info in a hurry and expect prompt and pleasant support from association staff. FAQs should be easily located on the organization's website. Responses to direct communications should provide specific answers and reference the site for future use. Be absolutely sure association staff can easily locate and refer to the FAQs.

41. Provide staff with responses to immediate issues and questions.

When issues arise that trigger member inquires, ensure that all necessary staff understand that issue and know the appropriate response to an inquiry. Developing a consistent response and communication style gives the caller or emailer a sense of confidence in that association's ability to find and communicate solutions.

42. Think before you place a phone call.
Fact: seven out of ten times, the person you're calling won't be available. Worse, when your call is finally returned, there's only a 30 percent chance *you'll* be available. When you call someone, presume they won't be in and plan a message before you dial.

43. Schedule a "phone meeting" in advance.
The person will be present and expecting your call. The best defense is a good offense.

44. Do you hear, but fail to listen?
Have you ever forgotten the other person's name because you are thinking about your next meeting? Pay attention to his or her words and read between the lines to understand the caller's true concern. Don't make assumptions about the caller's concerns; instead listen, clarify, and solve.

45. Be honest.
If you know little or nothing about the topic your member is addressing, be honest and ask for details so you can understand, investigate, and solve. Never guess the answer, but do let the caller know that you are working to find an answer or solution.

46. Be present in the conversation. Your distraction can be felt by the member and perceived negatively.
Trying to simultaneously finish a report, give hand signals to a co-worker, and approve a check request while taking a call or drafting an email is not only rude, it will likely to lead to some level of misunderstanding.

47. Emotions make you deaf.
Sociologists say that people instinctively begin to "fight" at the moment someone else opposes their point. They begin planning a counterattack, a process that obliterates good communication because the "fighter" just ends up tuning out the other person. Focus on the solution, not the problem.

48. Be professional.
What you don't say can be every bit as important as what you do say. Don't provide gossipy news, don't give out irrelevant or confidential information, don't divulge plans that haven't materialized, and don't discuss finances unless it is appropriate. Good rule: When in doubt, don't.

49. Address members by name and provide your name.
Get the caller's name early on, write it down, and use it often in the conversation. At the same time, make sure the member has your name and contact information. Make the conversation personal and positive.

50. Repeat instructions, introductions, and requests.
It's easy to tell how well someone has been listening if you ask them to repeat back to you what you've just said. It works the other way, too.

51. Remain in the present.
Your brain processes your thoughts four to ten times faster than people speak; so while they're talking, be careful that you're not thinking about what's for dinner. You know when you're "there" and when you're not. Tone of voice, eye contact, and response time are all important.

52. Confirm your response was understood.
Make a practice of confirming that you have answered the question or provided a solution before ending the conversation. All you have to say is, "Have I answered all of your questions?" or "Are we all set then?" The last words you speak are always the ones most remembered by the member. This little technique will give both you and the member a positive sense of closure.

53. Variety is key.
Don't just use one or two methods of communication. Say it often, say it differently, and say it at different times. Use web, newsletter, print, email, social networking, and announcements. Members don't always rely on one method of communication.

54. Send personal thank you notes for large purchases, completion of big projects by volunteers, or other activities that warrant it.

It's a nice touch and can be reinforcement for recognition.

There are many different and engaging ways to show appreciation to your members. The International Society for Pharmaceutical Engineering celebrates an annual Volunteer Appreciation Week, during which the organization sends a personal letter out to all of its volunteers worldwide. ISPE also gives committee members a 50 percent discount off all education fees, and the organization recognizes their efforts at an annual leadership dinner at the main conference.

Adapted from: Weaver Engel, Elizabeth. "Increase Member Engagement With Volunteer Recognition Programs." *Membership Developments*, September 2008.

55. When a member calls, go above and beyond the standard.

If they have a question and you offer the answer, see if you can't go beyond that. Here's an example: "I was wondering about registration for the fall event?" Your response: "Yes, I can help you with that. Be sure to make your reservations. Here is the number. If you'd like I can send you restaurants, activities, and other good information about the destination. Is there anything else that you need help with?"

56. Call unhappy members.

If someone is overheard or gave negative feedback online or via email, take the opportunity to turn the tides or at least hear the person out. Half the battle is listening and allowing members to improve their own experience. If you don't know about the problems, there is no way you could consider fixing them. Negative feedback can help your organization improve. The member's frustration may also be a result of not knowing all the options and not feeling heard. You can't assume every member knows every benefit or resource available. Take the time to find out what's truly bothering the member—there may be a viable solution.

57. Develop a web guide.

If you have a member center and/or complicated website, develop an easy to follow web guide that will help your members find what they need online and/or even give them suggestions on benefits they wouldn't normally tap in to.

58. Keep a call log to ensure good follow through.
If you can make notes in their membership records, it shows the next person what kind of communication has been happening with these members.

59. Distribute member alerts.
If there is hot news or urgent changes in the industry, develop a way to communicate that to your members. Find out how members want to receive news alerts (text, e-mail, Facebook?). Be careful not to bombard members with messages, and make sure you use subject lines that are specific enough to enable members to decide if your message is of immediate interest or can wait until later.

Adapted from: Rudick, Marilynne and O'Flahavan, Leslie. "4 Simple Rules for Writing Subject Lines." *Communication News*, August 2008.

Subject Lines That Sell

Your subject lines have to work doubly hard when you're writing for member email blasts or promoting a service, product, or event. Remember these rules for "must-open" promotional subject lines:

- **Feature benefits.** Make sure your subject line broadcasts a member benefit. For example, "25% off new subscriptions" is more powerful than "Special offer for new subscribers."

- **Make it short.** To increase your open rate, craft a subject line with fewer than 35 characters. Metrics compiled by MailerMailer found that these shorter subject lines had an open rate 28 percent higher than longer ones.

- **Avoid come-ons.** Don't use teasers ("Special offer—limited time!") that require the reader to click to find out what you're promoting. Readers find it annoying to have to click and wait for the message to open to find out what you're offering. Bottom line: They won't bother opening if you make them wait.

From "4 Simple Rules for Writing Subject Lines." *Communication News*, August 2008. www.asaecenter.org/Resources/ENewsletterCommunicationNews.cfm?ItemNumber=35838

60. When you engage members, sincerity is a hard thing to fake.

The art of conversation is through the practice of hearing and listening. You must hear your members and assure them that you are listening. Your actions will show that you understand. This sincerity and ability to truly empathize and converse with your member will create value.

61. Adapt.

Instill trust and confidence within your membership by active listening, hearing, action, change, and responsiveness.

The traditional association model is not designed to be nimble, and people are often afraid of the word "change," associating it with a painful process. It is important to approach everything as an opportunity to change and improve, and to create a flexible culture that allows people to try new things, make mistakes, and envision innovative outcomes.

Adapted from: "Critical Considerations for a Flexible Organization." Resources from the Knowledge Center, September 2009.

62. Be transparent.

Embrace all stimulus and feedback. Instead of deflecting or disregarding negative feedback, embrace it. Practice genuine, unbiased, nonjudgmental communication so that you can provide solutions to potential issues or at the least explanations or clarifications.

63. Create a primary contact response sheet for your organization.

Using your FAQs, identify the person/primary contact responsible for certain departments, committees, and/or projects. This way if the person who takes on the initial conversation with the member is asked a more in-depth question, there is someone to refer him or her to without requiring all first responders to know so much.

64. Empower front line responders to easily find answers to problems by creating a binder, look-up manual, or database that will allow them to search for key terms.

Then provide simple solutions and/or information that will enable the responder to direct the member in the proper manner.

65. Keep your cool when the going gets tough.

There is never—repeat, never—a reason for a staff member to swear at a member, no matter how abusive the behavior. At times like these, calmly remove yourself from the conversation and bring in your supervisor to take over.

66. "It's not our policy."

When a member makes a request that conflicts with an established association policy (unless it's truly impossible), say, "It's normally not our policy, but we'll try to make an exception in your case." Then see if you can, and make it happen if it's humanly possible. Always try to avoid making members feel like just another number in your database.

67. "I don't know."

Avoid this at all costs. "Let me find out; I'll provide a response within 24 hours" lets the member know that action is being taken.

68. "It's out of my control."

That may be true for the rep, but whatever it is, it's under *somebody's* control. Instead, say, "Let me double-check with our membership director (or whomever) to see what kind of solution we can find for you."

Education

69. Education requirements do not have to equal boring.

While you may still need to offer inexpensive e-learning programs to a segment of your membership for sustainability or revenue purposes, there is almost certainly a segment of your membership who are expecting more and who are waiting for you to provide it. This segment is your future. Find out who they are, what they are doing that's interesting to them, and what types of learning programs excite them. Often when given a choice for continuing education activity, members will prefer better over free and more engaging over short, meets-the-needs programs.

70. Remember that you're their alma mater.
Members came to you before to earn a credential or join a membership of professionals. Now focus on providing them with the tools and resources to build on that initial covenant. You have a history of expertise with a body of knowledge; bring that history with you into your member community's future.

71. Relevancy, not sales, is the key metric to track.
Nondues revenue is obviously important. However, securing short-term cash flow at the expense of value for your members will not build sustainable nondues revenue streams. Sales and volume will come in higher numbers with a more concerted effort to increase the relevancy of products.

72. Personalize the value of learning.
People no longer rely on their association as the only source of information on their profession. And when they do go to their association's website, many are faced with the task of hunting through web pages, catalogues, and PDF documents to find what's important to them. Try to help push the formats and styles that are important to your members by using their personal profiles already available in your AMS or other system of record.

73. Deliver your brand and member promise.
Every learning program you offer is an extension of your brand and promise. Be innovative, repurpose intellectual property, evolve your body of knowledge, employ new technologies, and keep the customer promise clear and reliable.

74. Leverage your learning community as a source of content advancement.
The old model of a speaker on stage or a talking head on synched slides does not contribute to a connected member community; in fact, it erodes it. There are many innovative examples of how groups of people have come together to create new content, ideas, and ways of advancing a profession through the effective use of technology.

75. Create attendee interaction at events or online by introducing a compelling catalyst.

Great simulations have a trigger or catalyst that unleashes a sense of urgency: a train derails, your keynote speaker is a no-show, your association merges with a competitor, or your young professionals special interest group (SIG) wants to start its own association. Select a simulation premise that can be succinctly stated but suggests a torrent of challenges and decisions for participants to confront and manage.

76. Create attendee interaction at events or online by role playing.

Appropriately defined roles help participants lose themselves in their parts, engaging their natural thinking and interaction tendencies. Provide participants detailed descriptions of their roles, but still leave room for interpretation and improvisation. Simulation facilitators often meet with participants to ensure roles are understood before launching the actual session. In some cases, a limited number of critical roles might be enacted by facilitators or other individuals not drawn from the participant ranks.

77. Location! Location! Location!

These three simple words can often determine engagement opportunities for your members. Sometimes unavoidable, but definitely something to keep in mind is the location of your face-to-face meetings. Make every attempt to rotate your big or small meetings as well as your committee meetings in various regions. Offer when feasible a virtual component so that your members who may not be able to travel can still engage and participate. If you have international members or are developing an international presence, this especially holds true. Be mindful of your cost/benefit ratio, but be creative and innovative to create meetings when and where your members can attend and engage with others.

78. Waive it.

Sometimes, unwritten policies are the best retention tools. For example, most associations have an inexplicably high application fee, which ostensibly covers the cost of "processing," whatever that is. On occasion, an astute potential member will see through this and call, demanding a waiver of the fee. Do it, even if there's nothing written down anywhere that says it's OK to do it. It doesn't happen very often, and you'll destroy the alienating, bureaucratic facade so many associations portray to new members. Besides, people love to get something for nothing, even though you're not losing anything by waiving the fee.

79. Do an email report card.

An innovative association in the far West asks its members to grade its performance each week by emailing in a one-page report card. The report cards have helped focus the association on what's important: the member's perception. The staff asks for feedback in four key areas: quality, delivery, communication, and service. Members receive the report card on the first Monday of the month and send it back by the first Friday of the month. Members fill in a numerical rating from zero to 100 and brief supporting comments on each of the four performance criteria; the comments will give you the reason why a rating may not be not good, so pay close attention to those. This simple system alerts managers to problems early on, when they can be more easily addressed. Most members participate, and they know their concerns are heard. A summary of each month's results is posted on the main association bulletin board and the website for all to see.

80. Find something that isn't broken and break it.

Is there a cheaper way to process transactions? Is there a more creative way to inform members of mundane information? Could you redesign a form to make it easier to fill out? Can you devise a simpler voicemail greeting? How about a better script for collection calls?

81. Note each call in each member's record.

Set up your computer system/database such that you can note the date and nature of the call, to whom the caller spoke, the request, and the response. This information can be used to highlight trends as well as providing a more intimate portrait of individual queries. Use this information to understand your members' concerns and needs and provide better service

82. Make your voicemail system caller friendly.

Your voicemail system can convey disinterest in the caller's issues when it is complicated and "unfriendly." The system should be as direct as possible, with short messages and clear directions.

83. Make your association voice mailbox message brief and easy.

Build your recorded message branching based on the most frequently contacted department and/or referenced topic: "You have reached the ABC Association. For membership, press 1. For the accounting office, press 2. For other departments or personal assistance, please press 0." Two levels of instructions should be the limit. Please avoid complicated directories.

84. A dissatisfied member is the ultimate consultant.

You're probably already acquainted with your more vocal members, the ones who are so willing to give you an earful about what you're doing wrong, what you're not doing, and what you should be doing. As irritating as the curmudgeonly member can be, his or her comments are valuable and can almost always teach you something. If you're willing to turn your dissatisfied members into membership consultants, you can effectively fix problems many others are probably suffering silently. Utilize the member's passion on a subject and channel their energy to volunteer for the group and/or spearhead a project to fix the problem.

85. "Silent complainers."

What can you do about the members who have serious complaints, but remain silent? It's a real problem because the member has left you thinking you're doing an adequate job when in fact, you're openly antagonizing him or her. It's no one's fault; the member's responsibility is to speak up if dissatisfied. Part of your job is to try to anticipate that dissatisfaction and head it off. A few suggestions: forthright surveys that openly encourage members to speak up (written surveys provide more anonymity); "proving" to the membership that you respond to their concerns via an association-wide communication; random calls, especially to members from whom you don't normally hear.

86. How do you know how you're providing good member service?

The TQM/CQI rage from two decades ago has simmered down a bit, but many associations took to heart the core concept: be the best you can be and find a way to document it so you can measure your performance and continue improving. There are many, many, finite, detailed and esoteric principles in TQM/CQI, which can cause a variety of problems, mostly of the budgetary kind. These principles don't all apply to every circumstance, and some of them are virtually impossible to implement in certain situations, though proponents will tell you that you must follow the principles to the letter or it won't work. Take the pieces of TQM that appeal to you (and are practical, of course) and put them to work for you; most importantly, you must identify the measurable aspects of tasks and activities. A standard of "is efficient" isn't good enough; "Error rate is less than 1 percent" is measurable.

87. Do a systems check.

When your association forces members to conform or learn your systems, then those systems are automatically not meeting member needs. If you're saying things like "We can't do that," "That's not how things work here," or "You'll have to wait until Monday—that's when Joe gets back from vacation," your systems are working against your members.

88. Use secret shoppers to find out if the service being provided is adequate.

Identify areas of weakness online and at in-person at events. The Automotive Oil Change Association provides a mystery-shopping program for members that provides a report rating the shop's performance and giving feedback about negative observations.

Mystery shopping can help monitor your competition, assure your shop's brand is being followed, catch an employee doing something wrong—or right, analyze trends, and identify training opportunities.

Adapted from: Vanover Porter, Margo. "We've Got a Secret." *Associations Now,* July 2006.

89. Identify trends in the industry and/or government that may affect members.

You should be helping them see their future. ASAE & The Center for Association Leadership conducts ongoing environmental scans to identify trends affecting the association community. The trends can guide association staff to understand where their industry is heading as they manage the strategic planning process.

Adapted from: Buhr, Samantha. "Developing Strategies With Future Trends." *AMC Connection,* September 2006.

90. Look at membership value not through your members' eyes but through their customers' eyes.

If you can tap into what is needed for members to better serve their customers, you may add benefits that are truly valuable to members.

91. Wear your member's shoes?

Yep. Consider yourself in their role. Think about needs, their perspective and their overall experience. What solution can you solve for them? How can you make them feel more connected when attending a meeting for the first time and may not know any other attendees? Keep the human factor in mind.

92. Create recognizable brand and stick with it.

A strong brand will help your members identify projects that the organization is putting together. Strong brand engagement correlates to strong financial performance.

93. Identify keywords that are pivotal to your organization.

The list should include brand, products, industry lingo and buzzwords, names of competitors, competitive products, and industry terms. Use Boolean search techniques and implement these words into your documents, web pages, video titles, and/or anything else that is searchable. This allows people who are searching for materials to find your organization.

94. Never stop!

Provide stellar customer service and never conclude that you can't do even better. We often become complacent when our membership satisfaction surveys come back positive and our members pat us on the back for a job well done. Continue to give your members the best customer service and always maintain your professional standards.

COMPONENTS

95. Segment communications and target engagement opportunities to different components based upon that component's needs.

For example, don't send a message about shoveling snow off the roof in winter to the realtor associations in the south.

96. To successfully engage a member on the component level, determine the level of commitment from the person's supervisor.

Try to engage the supervisor in the activity or group to generate buy-in. If the supervisor cannot participate, make sure he or she understands the value of the employee being active.

97. When an individual indicates interest in the organization, have someone from the local or area component connect with the person via email, a phone call, or a tweet.

Local members can answer questions and share why they feel the organization is valuable.

There is tremendous value in building personal and authentic relationships with individual members. Create opportunities for new members to connect with active, local members. Ask a member from a successful component to mentor a new component's leader. Ask members in the chapters throughout your organization for opinions on your conferences, publications or website—and ask in a public forum where others can join in. Members will be grateful that your association offers them valuable networking opportunities.

Adapted from: Coffman, Kylee. "Build Authentic Relationships With Your Chapters." *Component Relations*, October 2010.

98. Clearly define the project or activity that you want the person to engage in at the local level, including the amount of time that it will take.

Also, outline how the activity will impact them directly on their local or regional level. For example, before asking members to write to their U.S. Senators about a national issue, determine how that issue affects them locally.

99. Attend a chapter meeting to show involvement and support of the chapter.

Not only does your attendance show involvement and support, it also presents you with a great opportunity to learn more about the needs of the chapter and their members and what products or services would interest them. Armed with this newfound knowledge, you can develop or modify offerings that will resonate with them and increase their engagement with the national organization.

MARKETING

100. Create an economic relief program.

Offer discounts on products, free webinars for members, free shipping, or free whitepapers. Stimulate their interests by giving things away. Waiving dues for members up for renewal who are temporarily out of work can be a benefit that converts them to an engaged, lifelong member. Simplify your categories of membership and dues structure to make it easier for new members to try your services.

101. Offer a free trial on membership benefits online.

Encourage prospects to get involved. Be diverse. Make sure that you take into consideration the diversity of your membership in terms of generation, professional background, and income. Incorporate that

Membership Structures Then and Now

Commercial Finance Association

- *PREVIOUS MEMBERSHIP STRUCTURE:* Closed membership, only available to lenders at the national and chapter levels.

- *NEW MEMBERSHIP STRUCTURE:* Open membership, available to lenders at the national level and to service providers, lenders, and nonlenders at the chapter level.

American College of Healthcare Executives

- *PREVIOUS MEMBERSHIP STRUCTURE:* Three levels of membership: Member, Diplomate (CHE), and Fellow (FACHE)—each requiring different educational degrees and levels of expertise/experience.

- *NEW MEMBERSHIP STRUCTURE:* Two levels of membership: Member and Fellow (FACHE)—with additional educational requirements for the FACHE credential.

National Volunteer Fire Council

- *PREVIOUS MEMBERSHIP STRUCTURE:* Fire department memberships available for $50 plus $30 per volunteer member.

- *NEW MEMBERSHIP STRUCTURE:* "All-Staff Membership" available with no fee for department membership and $10 per volunteer member.

Professional Association of Innkeepers International

- *PREVIOUS MEMBERSHIP STRUCTURE:* Member dues based on number of rooms in the member's inn, starting at $215 for one to five rooms.

- *NEW MEMBERSHIP STRUCTURE:* Three levels of membership/member dues: Silver starting at $89, Gold starting at $199, and Platinum starting at $289.

Reprinted from "Rethink Your Membership Structure" from *Associations Now,* August 2010. http://www.asaecenter.org/Resources/ANowDetail. cfm?ItemNumber=51781 into your marketing and messaging. Find out what each group really wants.

Trying out an unconventional dues structure can yield surprising results. For example, the American Dental Education Association eliminated individual dues in 2006, and membership increased sevenfold in just a few months. As a result of this radical change at ADEA, member engagement, advocacy, meeting attendance, and even paid institutional membership have all grown.

Adapted from: Krug, Susan and Abigail Gorman. "No Dues, More Members." *Associations Now,* December 2010.

102. Globalization is a major factor affecting the future of membership.

If you are not yet interacting with communities that have similar missions, you need to incorporate strategies that effectively serve the outer community. Don't let geographic location define how you interact internationally or outside your area. For example, when Viagara came on the market, Japan and Europe blocked distribution of the product until other companies in their area could develop similar products. What they didn't anticipate was that the public, through globalization and technology, was able to get the product by getting prescriptions from doctors online and getting it shipped directly from the United States. Not only did they miss out on the taxes and revenue, their vision was limited because they thought they could control their environment. Consider a virtual membership that will allow access to your organization from outside your typical membership boundaries.

103. Make it EASY.

Execution of member processes in any virtual/online platform is critical to their engagement. Want to keep a member engaged and coming back to your website? Purchasing online products? Or signing up, completing a survey or any other transacting process online with you? Make sure the process is secure and your instructions, terms, and conditions are easy to understand. And see to it the process has few clicks, doesn't overwhelm them in copy or text, and you have easy-to-reach and fast tech support follow-up in case of a problem.

104. Track your members' purchases.

If you have a customer relationship management system, "smart" database, handwritten ledger, or simple punch card, track your members' purchases. This level of intelligence can help you tailor your messages, highlighting various services, products, or events that are relevant to their needs. This "Amazon.com" environment helps to keep your members aware and encourages them to become repeat purchasers of products.

105. Track member participation.

Along the line of tracking member purchases, consider tracking member participation. Knowing how active or inactive, involved or uninvolved a member is can help your organization better determine a course of action or communication.

106. Provide and encourage the use of your logo.

This is especially a powerful message for those segments of your membership that provide some sort of service to your members. In addition to helping to build member loyalty, it also signifies and promotes peer recognition.

107. Develop an "industry" space on your website or communications corner in your print or electronic news to recognize your members.

Your organization consists of the movers and the shakers in your industry. Be sure to recognize them. When members are recognized for their achievements and activities, it demonstrates that the organization is interested in them. Additionally, carving out a space to recognize their achievements creates an opportunity to get your members' attention and gives them a reason to visit your site and share with others. How might you capture this information? Consider using Google alerts or other social media alert mechanisms.

108. Redesign your membership card to include information that outlines ways to make the most of your membership offerings.

Consider making it a downloadable document your members can get when they go to your website.

Examples of Benefit Offerings

The ASAE: The Center for Association Leadership website **www.asaecenter.org** has numerous examples you can access of how other organizations inform members of benefits offerings. "Membership Tools and Resources: Benefits Flyers" is a Models & Samples resource that provides links to the membership flyers of 25 associations (available for members when logged in at **www.asaecenter.org/ Resources/modelslist.cfm?ItemNumber=12296**).

Consider the successes of other organizations to find the most engaging ways to inform members of the services you provide.

109. Provide discounts after purchases.

Much like the reward "bucks" offered through many retail stores, consider providing discounts as a reward after your member makes a purchase. This not only articulates that you are thankful for their purchase, but it also encourages them to come back to you for future needs. The "discounts" can be substituted to allow access to special events or an upgrade to an upcoming event or meeting.

110. If you offer a reward program of some sort, be sure to evaluate it.

Is it achieving the goals you had in mind? Think about, too, whether you're giving freebies to those members who would have bought anyway. This is important to keep in mind so that you don't "devalue" your products or services or impact your profit margin. You want to maintain your profitability so that you can continue offering quality services to your members.

111. Develop group-engagement opportunities and pricing.

Many group-buying sites have emerged. Consider borrowing this concept by developing engagement opportunities for your members at the same organization. Collective engagement opportunities can also be geared to members of various segments of your membership. If you have an upcoming program or event and would like to increase participation from your Gen Xers or Y's, create an opportunity for them to sign up collectively for your activities or events.

ENGAGEMENT

What is member engagement?

"...capturing the attention, affiliation, and loyalty of members by giving them what they need through highly relevant value-building activities."

> – *Membership Essentials*, p. 206

Engagement is about value—the value for the person doing the engaging as well as the value of that engagement for the association. Engagement is evidence of success and provides fuel for your mission and future growth. Members and others investing in the association demonstrate perceived high value. Properly structured, such investment will give the organization the financial and human capital it needs to achieve goals and maximize contributions to its mission.

Why should you care?

- Involved members don't drop out. However, before they become involved, they need to become engaged.
- Meaningful connections and experiences for your members will keep them coming back.
- It costs five to six times more to recruit a new member than it does to keep an existing one.

Start your engagement plan by breaking it down into pre-membership (non-member) engagement and post-membership application engagement. This helps you target the right audience for each of your engagement ideas and plans. Track these ideas to ensure a positive success rate.

Pre-membership:

- Viewing content on your website, blog, Twitter feed, Facebook fan page, and so forth
- Paying attention to a PSA or press coverage
- Sharing content from your website or other publication
- Buying a product
- Attending a conference or event
- Applying for a job via your career center

Examples of post-membership application engagement could include all of the above, as well as:

- Writing or speaking
- Volunteering for a committee or task force
- Serving in a leadership role
- Receiving recognition such as fellowship or other achievement status
- Spending significant money on sponsorship, advertising, exhibit space, and so forth
- Spreading the word about the value of the association and recruiting new members

Welcoming New Members

112. Make welcome calls to new members.

New members receiving welcome calls are delighted by an unexpected surprise, especially in this age of electronic communication. This personal touch can help your association build a stronger understanding of why people join and what benefits are most valuable as well as providing opportunities to develop new offerings. By initiating a two-way dialogue with your members, you start to move the dial from a transaction of joining the association into a relationship.

Depending on the size of your association, you may not have the staff resources to make welcome phone calls. In this case, you can turn to your volunteers to help. Try recruiting ambassadors to welcome members in their geographic area, area of expertise, etc. Ideally, there needs to be a mechanism for the volunteers to communicate information received, questions, or items for follow-up to the association staff.

113. Connect new members with partners to get them introduced to the association.
Their partners can explain how they leveraged the benefits of membership in their careers and help them identify opportunities to collaborate and network with other members either virtually or face-to-face.

114. Encourage new members to join a component, special interest group, or community of practice.
Connecting new members to others with similar areas of interest and possibly facing the same challenges provides the member with a better sense of belonging and increases his or her comfort level. It also increases the likelihood he or she will participate or at least gain value as a lurker within the group.

115. Conduct new member orientation online and at face-to-face events.
Plan an activity that helps members meet each other, such as ice breakers or speed networking. Invite veteran members to the orientation to provide their insights into making the most of membership and to network. Create a memorable experience for your new members.

116. Engage new members using high-touch techniques.
Membership benchmarking research indicates that high-touch new member contacts like mailed welcome kits, volunteer or staff welcome calls, new member surveys, and new member receptions seem to correlate with better renewal rates.

117. The most important time to engage a member is when they first join an association.
Once a member joins, he or she becomes the most likely member not to renew. Almost every association finds that it has the lowest renewal rate among first-year members. That's why many

associations call the first year of membership the "conversion year" and add special programs to engage new members.

118. Provide a new member kit that contains documents and/or products.

These materials provide a good introduction to your organization and also provide a method for cross-marketing events/products. Make follow-up phone calls. Make sure they have received their new member kits and/or confirmations

119. Set up new member events or tables at meetings.

This helps new members meet others and allows them to feel engaged and welcome.

The Medical Group Management Association has offered a new-member reception at their annual conference to help first-time attendees navigate the event and get the most out of the networking and educational opportunity. MGMA sent new members a special invitation to meet other new members, become more familiar with the organization, and spend time with board members. The new-member reception was held on the first day of the conference. The goal was to impart a professional, friendly impression of the conference and the association.

Adapted from: Webster, Kris and Meryl Glickman. "A Star-Studded Event." *Membership Developments*, September 2003.

120. Identify new members and first-time attendees at your meetings.

Ask your board, committee, and staff members to engage with these members that have the ribbons, special decals, or some other identifier. Target key volunteers that you know will go out of their way to help welcome them.

121. Recognize new members.

Feature them in your publications and/or at events. Recognize new members for their first or second anniversaries. Depending upon your budget, this could be a pin, a letter from the chairman, or newsletter recognition—a gesture that shows you appreciate their involvement. A new member who receives a letter from your executive director will feel singled out and appreciated.

Adapted from: Barrett, Miranda. "Show Them the Love: Seven Easy Ways to Show Members You Care." *Membership Developments*, December 2010.

122. Provide a directory of the membership broken down by last name, geographic area, specialty or other area of interest.
This will help them to network and find a common denominator that they feel comfortable with.

123. Identify your board of directors and committee members.
Let your members know who their leadership is so there is an identifiable face for their concerns when it comes to the direction of the association or organization.

124. Develop a new member map/plan.
You should be following a guide on how to regularly engage new members so that their first-year experience will be great.

125. Offer special interest group signup on your membership application.
It gets new members involved earlier. Then match new members with an experienced mentor with the same interests and follow up to be sure the new member has been able to make useful connections.

Engaging Members Through Benefits and Services

PREPARING MEMBERS FOR THE FUTURE

126. Establish collaborative communities organized by specialty, geography, or career stage.
For virtual groups, there are a variety of online tools available that can be fully integrated with your association management system, as well as free or inexpensive services from companies such as Google, Yahoo, Ning, and Groupsite.

127. Organize credentialing study groups.

Components can help organize them locally. For example, the exam for the prestigious Certified Association Executive credential has always been tough, so ASAE and local SAEs offer study groups that help candidates use fellow association professionals to prepare. Whether it's an offline study group, a social network, or a Google Group, your association can support members to succeed in the credentialing process. ASAE offers a full-featured CAE Candidate SharePoint site. In addition to networking with other candidates or CAEs, candidates can download scores of test-prep resources, such as domain-specific documents, flash-card sets and practice exams.

Adapted from: Laxton, Christopher, E. "Online Resources for CAE Preparation," July 2010.

128. Recruit volunteer "career advisors" for students and new professionals.

There are a variety of ways they can provide advice: talking to members one-on-one, developing articles or tips for your website, and facilitating online discussions about career opportunities.

129. Institute a mentoring program.

For every new member, young professional, or aspiring student who would participate in the program and benefit from the counsel of someone who has been through the ropes, you create two engagement opportunities—the mentor and the mentee. Registration does not need to be a sophisticated online process. It can be as simple as the association keeping a list of volunteers willing to serve as mentors and connecting them with individuals who contact the organization wanting to be assigned a mentor.

130. Consider a traditional method.

Visit your members at their office. Consider placing more emphasis on those members that are least active. Your staff may have the opportunity to reach out to members within your city. However, take advantage of those trips outside of your city as an opportunity to connect with your members. Identify those members that are not as active or who may have only one person as a member from their office and visit.

131. Offer exclusive members-only webinars, content, resources, and events.

Provide solutions to challenges your members are facing. First survey members to understand what resources they value, then give them access to online publications and other content, and create opportunities for them to network with one another and with industry experts.

132. Celebrate your members' milestone anniversaries.

Any time you can add the personal touch and recognize members individually, do so. The difference between personal contact and individual recognition versus generic communication or treating them as a number within a group are miles apart. If you were Jane Doe, which would you rather see in your association's magazine? "We had three members reach their 10-year membership anniversary in July" or "We would like to recognize and thank Jane Doe, Joe Public, and Harry Wotsit for reaching their 10-year membership anniversary and for the contributions they've made to our profession during that time."

133. Understand the demographic composition of your membership so you can tailor your communications, volunteer opportunities, and benefits to meet their needs.

Look at generational traits, career stages, geography, gender, and other demographics. Examine segments within your membership that are unique to your association, such as their specialty area, level within their workplace (mid-level manager, executive), profession (for vertical associations), or industry (in horizontal organizations).

How will these variables affect member engagement in the association? Members who are young, fresh out of school, and hungry to start their career may have different motivations compared to mid-career members when they look for opportunities to participate in association activities. How does the generation factor influence communication?

134. Social networking: If you don't do it, someone else will.

Include social networking in your vehicles of communication. The more varied your communication, the more your message will be reinforced.

A Listening Toolkit

Maggie McGary explains what tools she uses for her listening process:

- Search blogs and locate members who are blogging: Technorati, Google BlogSearch, and Google Alerts.
- Track keywords and locate members using Twitter: Tweetbeep, Twitter search, and Twilerts.
- Read lots of blogs about social media: A few favorites are Inside Facebook, Social Media Musings by Tom Humbarger, and Association Jam. A good starting point is Alltop's social media category.
- Follow social media people on Twitter: A few are Jeremiah Owyang (@jowyang), Pete Cashmore (@mashable), and Lynn Morton (@MissLynn13). To view all the people McGary follows, you can check the list on her Twitter profile, @maggielmcg.
- Subscribe to newsletters and online publications: Ragan's Daily Headlines, Social Media Today, SocialFishing, Smart Publishing, SmartBrief on Social Media, MarketingProfs Daily, and AdAge Digital.
- Use video alerts to find videos made by or featuring members.
- Join several social networks and use them a lot to bounce ideas off other people and to hear about what other organizations are doing—what's working and what's not.

Her words of wisdom: "Because social media is always evolving and new tools are constantly surfacing (or dying), this position is one that really requires a dedicated, ongoing commitment to professional development and a pretty substantial investment of nonwork time reading and networking."

From "A Listening Toolkit," *Associations Now,* November 2009. http://www.asaecenter.org/Resources/ANowDetail.cfm?ItemNumber=45789

135. Whether it's Twitter, Facebook, LinkedIn or YouTube, don't just define your level of success as the number of friends and/or activity.

Try to be present. Use social networking to start discussions and/or introduce topics that may be of interest to members. Post meeting activities and pictures on your sites. These sites serve as hubs between the organization and its customers. Social networking creates customer-focused engagement.

136. Develop a social media timeline.

Establish the current state of your brand within each network, recommend a 30-day review period where you can implement different strategies, and see what works after each 30-day period.

137. Post items on your website that encourage viewing and/or web activity.

Make sure that your website is current and constantly changing. Post archives of newsletters, articles, and white papers to offer more opportunity to engage with your website.

138. Search engine optimization.

Make sure your website is searchable. Members, prospects, and others who have questions about your field of interest should be able to run general searches that will lead back to your organization.

139. Allow job postings and classified ads on your website.

Job announcements and classifieds are a good way to keep members aware of the job market and climate for their profession or industry. It also gives them an opportunity to post jobs and/or products they want to promote.

140. Your online staff directory should include pictures and contact information.

Give members the personal touch. Include information about staff areas of expertise and personal interests; ask staff to include the title of the best association- or industry-related book they've read. Members will enjoy being able to put a face and some personal information to a voice they hear on the phone or a name in an email message.

141. Be sure that the wisdom of the crowds found online concerning your organization and/or field of interest leads back to you.

For example, monitor Wikipedia, about.com, Fotopedia, Spock, and others to make sure that these sites that the public often turns to for information at the very least mentions your organization and correct information about it.

142. Post pictures and videos.

Pictures and videos are a great vehicle for showing other members being engaged. This encourages participation.

143. Make more content available.

Content is necessary to drive activity. You must have your content present and searchable to maximize your engagement.

144. Be flexible.

New media is constantly changing and evolving. What works today may not work tomorrow, so keep current.

145. Consider livecasting events.

Those who are unable to attend a meeting have the option of joining a live cast via audio or video in real-time.

146. Engagement through online platforms doesn't revolve around training or knowledge of the software or platform.

If there is content and value within that platform, most members will adapt and learn in order to access the knowledge. Focus on the value and not what you need to do to get people to engage.

147. Consider the app world.

Some of your members may be "app happy." Consider developing a free app they can download on their phones or computer that allows them to select the information they want and learn ways to make the most of their membership experience.

148. Consider a "My *(name of your organization)*" page.

Often times our websites are a daunting place filled with great information. Consider developing an interactive web page that allows your members to self-select their category and interests and receive information on how to make the most of their experience.

149. Develop a "Daily Tips" page.
For each day of the year, have a "tip" that allows your members to make the most of their membership experience by outlining various ways to engage or get more involved. The tips can be organized and segmented according to your membership segments or groups. Consider setting these tips to include RSS feed capability.

150. Develop a "preference center" for your members.
Let's face it, from time to time we all battle with what to send our members and how much should we send them. Consider incorporating a preference center on your website that allows your member to self-select topic codes or information they want or to opt in or out of some of your communications. This will help take the guess work out of what your members want and need and will give you a better a sense of topics are of interest to them.

151. A word of technical caution.
While employing awesome resources afforded by the new emerging technologies, take into consideration your members' technical acumen and the accessibility of these tools. If the tools and technology you are currently using, planning to use or wish to use requires downloading documents or installation of software, remember that some organizations may not provide administrative rights for their staff to do so on their company-issued computer or phone. If the service is being used on a mobile device take into account how it may look once the member downloads. Different mobile devices will display the content differently thus creating a totally different experience for the member.

Engaging Members Through Relationships

152. Map the member experience to identify areas needing improvement.

For example, you can examine the member experience for your annual conference from the time members register online to their arrival onsite and throughout the event.

153. Listen to members and the questions they are asking.

This can give you ideas for new programs and benefits to offer and help you identify what information to push to the top in your communications.

154. Conduct online surveys and polls.

Extensive research is important; however, one or two question polls can quickly generate targeted member feedback. Polls can be posted on your website, embedded in an e-newsletter, and posted on your association's Facebook page. Know your members. Conducting polls, surveys, or simply asking members their opinion keeps you aware of their needs.

155. Be sure to read and go through your evaluations.

Conducting the survey is not helpful unless you follow up and actually evaluate. Convene a task force or working group to evaluate feedback, identify action items, and make a plan to implement the changes members desire.

156. Let your membership know how their answers came through.

Let them know what the poll said and how the organization is responding. Do this in several ways by using newsletters, email, faxes, or announcements to communicate the information. It encourages them to keep contributing feedback.

157. Identify benefits that are no longer of value.

This is part of the culture of an ongoing evaluation and elimination assessment. Eliminating programs and benefits that are no longer valued by members will free up resources to allow you to focus on products, programs, or services more members will find valuable and worthy of engaging.

158. Survey the staff.

Your staff will know first hand what members complain about and/or praise. But don't just focus on the complaints and what you might do to reduce them. Both areas deserve reflection. Enhancements made to benefits that members praise can often be more valuable than fixing something that a few squeaky wheels voice their opinion about. Staff can be an excellent source of ideas for enhancing products or programs so be sure to inquire about enhancements in your staff survey.

159. Organize focus groups, either online or in person.

This can be a double win for the organization. In addition to the engagement points gained by involving members in focus groups and giving them the opportunity to provide feedback, if you can populate your focus group with subject matter experts (SMEs), then you can utilize their expertise to help guide the development and direction of a product or service. Members find great value in being able to contribute back to the profession.

160. Hold "hot topic" sessions.

These sessions would address challenges and opportunities your members are experiencing in the workplace or sector. Invite the members who participate in these sessions to blog about what's discussed at the meetings or contribute an article to your newsletter or other publications. This sends a message that you really care about members' opinions and may inspire other members to participate.

161. When in doubt, think Disney.

Make sure you're not only member-centric, but you appeal to all five senses. Keep in mind your members' sense of 1) need, 2) time, 3) budget, 4) reputation, and 5) ROI. If you want to go Disney, each opportunity that you have to appeal to all of your members' senses helps to make a memorable experience which in turn serves as encouragement for future engagement and involvement.

CREATE A COLLABORATIVE ENVIRONMENT

162. Facilitate collaborative writing projects on issues or concerns facing your members.

Try an online tool such as www.writeboard.com. This allows members to share information and discuss issues or concerns facing the industry.

163. Create a platform for informal idea-sharing sessions to swap tips related to your members' profession or area of interest.

This can be done online or in person, locally or nationally. Think about the objectives you want to achieve first, then work backwards to create the platform. For example, if your key objective is to get your members meeting face-to-face, then create a low- or no-cost program at the local level. To keep meeting costs down, ask your members or industry partners if they're willing to donate meeting space.

164. Don't be afraid to fail.

Obviously this is something you don't want to do all the time. However, by being afraid to fail, you're keeping yourself from the learning process that comes with failing. For instance, one association's first foray into social media using a Ning group for its conference attendees was a total failure. However, the association learned that it could achieve success by using a more known platform, such as Facebook, and engaging its members rather than waiting for them to engage themselves. While it may be difficult to fail, sometimes it's a necessary evil to learn what works best for your members.

165. Launch a member-get-a-member campaign.

Not only does this bring you new members, it engages your current members and rewards them for their efforts.

166. Invite members to be at your exhibit booth to meet and greet current members.

They can also talk to prospects about the value of membership based on their first-hand experience. Pre-record testimonials (another way to engage members!) that can play in your exhibit booth.

167. Develop a viral testimonial campaign.

Similar to a member-get-a-member campaign but utilizing social media tools, engage your members to share with others what they value the most from their membership. Upload their video, blog, tweet, status update, etc. about the top three things they value the most about their membership with your organization. Consider making the campaign into a contest and offer a prize such as a complimentary registration to one of your upcoming meetings or a complimentary product or service your organization currently offers to cross promote, build awareness around or promote future engagement opportunities.

168. Create a list of "one-hit wonders."

These are tasks that your members can do for you that require very little time. Examples include posting on LinkedIn or Facebook, distributing brochures, tweeting at a meeting, or writing a blog post.

169. Send an email to those members who normally aren't engaged.

Provide them with the opportunity to make a contribution to the association and make them feel that they are appreciated and valued as members.

170. Stay in contact.

Call once a year (mid year) so that the member knows that the only point of contact is not to collect dues. Send an annual list of benefits and how to access them.

171. Customize your messages.

If you can customize your message so that the member knows that you know them, this will pay off. Example: If you send a form letter that says Dear Member, it's better if you say Dear John or Mr. Smith. Additionally, mention their most recent activity: "It was great seeing you at the meeting. You last ordered brochures six months ago. How are your stock levels? This type of customization makes the relationship stronger.

172. Consider blog radio to keep your members informed.

This easy, inexpensive opportunity may be an ideal solution to organizations whose members tend to listen to internet radio while working. Include interviews by their peers, industry experts, HQ updates and, if you have components, updates from your various chapters. Include practical day-to-day tips your members can use to help them do their jobs but also consider adding simple solutions to help members strike a balance between their work and their personal lives.

173. Develop "gift cards" for members.

Award the cards to your members for efforts such as volunteering, writing an article, speaking at your events, or recruiting a new member. They could use your organization's gift card towards your events or meetings, or products and services offered by your organization. Include on the back of the card three short, quick steps that outline ways to engage with the organization including short URLs.

174. Give your members a Personalized URL (PURL).

Implement a PURL campaign to connect to your members. This technique includes a web address that includes a personal landing page for the member (Example: www.JohnDoe. AssociationXYZ. org). Organize your members' landing pages to include information that he or she expects and would resonate with his or her needs. How? Think AIR campaign. What sort of information would get your members **attention or attract** him/her. Next develop a component of your campaign that will generate interaction. The **interaction** could be built into their personalized landing page. Finally, you want to cause a **reaction** or, in some marketing 101 schools of thought, "a cause to action." Attention/Attraction. Interaction. Reaction. Make sure your PURL isn't a standalone outreach. PURLs are also great because you can track responses and gain more intelligence about your members.

175. Include internal ads in your publications that outline quick and easy ways to make the most of membership.

Consider in-house ads to help deliver key messages that outline ways your members can make the most of their membership experience with your organization. Budget in advance for this opportunity if you are concerned that this may take away from potential ad dollars.

176. Develop a member engagement calendar.

Plan and develop an engagement calendar for your members. Include a digital component as well if you would like to incorporate monthly campaigns or if there are any new services or activities your members can engage in through their membership. Word of caution, be sure to include some activities that do not cost your members an additional fee. This shouldn't be a "sales" pitch calendar. Also consider including vouchers or coupons for special events or programs. On certain days of each month highlight activities like: *check and update your membership profile or credentials, don't forget to sign up to volunteer, deadline for RFP or speaking opportunity is fast approaching! Contact your staff liaison to learn more ways to make the most of your membership!* Be sure to include short URLs if they wish to learn more and include staff contact information.

177. Make the ASK!

If you don't ask them, they won't ever come. Keep asking members to participate. If possible, make it a call and/or ask volunteers to reach out and make the ASK!

Moving Members from Engaged to Involved

VOLUNTEER RECOGNITION

178. Recognize your volunteers every chance you can get.
You can't say thank you enough to volunteers for giving of their time and expertise. Vary the methods you use to show appreciation: call-outs in your publications, letters from the executive director, announcing the list of "stars" at your events. All of these efforts let volunteers know that you notice and are grateful for their contribution.

179. Create a volunteer point system where they can earn points for involvement.
Recognize and redeem points often. Points can help you identify potential board members.

180. Awards and contests.
Offer ways for members to contribute and win awards and contests. For example, you could give an award for the best writing or highest number of article submission pages.

181. Highlight or profile members and volunteers who have made considerable contributions and/or achievements.
One way to do this is to create a Fellow category of membership. This identifies professionals that have achieved a higher standard of involvement and sets a goal for others to strive for.

182. Say "Thank You" to your volunteers.
For associations with mostly U.S. members, recognize your volunteers during National Volunteer Week, which is held each April through the Hands on Network.

183. Go beyond the usual suspects.
Recognize members who wrote a letter to a legislator, appeared in the press, and so forth. Appeal to members to report in about their association- and industry-related activities. This communicates to them that you're interested in and appreciate their efforts.

And reading about the small accomplishments of members may encourage others to play their own part in the organization.

184. Publicly recognize volunteer achievements.
Thank your members individually and as a group. Celebrate successes. Consider ways in which your chief staff executive can provide further recognition to volunteers, perhaps by dropping in to say hello at your face-to-face meeting.

VOLUNTEER OPPORTUNITIES

185. Welcome all volunteers and get them involved sooner than later.
Designate special projects or tasks for those whose commitment may not be long and/or have special skill sets that may be helpful.

186. Make it easy to get involved.
Volunteers shouldn't have to go through a long process to participate. Include short news items on your website about volunteer opportunities, and include an easy-to-use link that brings members to a user-friendly volunteer opportunities page.

187. Create committees or task forces for all events and projects.
Without creating too many subdivisions within your governance structure, look for as many ways as possible to engage volunteers.

188. Survey volunteers about their experience.
This will help you keep them engaged after a project is completed and give you good insight for improving future volunteer experiences.

189. Host a leadership orientation for board members and committee chairs.
Help new volunteers make the most of their leadership experience. This is a new role for many. Discuss expectations and provide them with resources that will help them fulfill their responsibilities.

190. Initiate an ambassador program.

Select members who are willing to represent the organization at public events and/or in front of other members.

191. Be flexible when creating volunteer opportunities.

In addition to more traditional committee participation that may require a big time commitment, create short- term, project-specific opportunities. Young professionals, in particular, may be more willing to get involved if the task is clearly defined and time-limited.

192. When recruiting volunteers, define the volunteer roles, time commitment, and duration.

Setting clear expectations in advance lends itself to a more rewarding experience and increases the likelihood of achieving the volunteer's goals and completing the project on time.

193. Be transparent in your volunteer selection process.

If you are looking for specific skill-sets, areas of expertise, or levels of experience, make that known upfront.

194. Look for opportunities to get students and new professionals involved.

Maybe it's a special membership category. Maybe it's creating relevant content that students or new professionals can access for free. Whatever opportunities you can think of, be sure you're capturing their pertinent information in your database so you can move them along your engagement pipeline to becoming an engaged, full-time member.

195. Provide your staff with training on working with volunteers and clearly define expectations.

Help them understand the subtle differences of managing or coordinating a "workforce" of volunteers compared to paid staff.

196. Define the role of staff and the type of support they will provide in the work being done by volunteers.

For example, a committee may be responsible for setting the policy and direction for a strategic initiative, while the staff oversees how it is executed and implemented.

197. Consider establishing an ongoing volunteer group to provide advice about a specific association product.

For example, start an editorial advisory board to provide input on the magazine or newsletter. Decide the scope of the group's role. Do you want the group to be a decision-making body or strictly an advisory body that provides input for staff to consider? Decide how many volunteers would work best for the group. Aim for a group large enough to provide diverse perspectives yet small enough to get results. Depending on the demographics of your association and the scope of your product, the ideal size for the group might be 6 to 12 individuals. Write the equivalent of a brief (no more than one page) job description to outline your expectations for the volunteers.

198. Articulate the role they will play and the tasks you would like them to perform.

When inviting members to consider the volunteer role, give them this document, walk them through it, and ask them to consider carefully whether they have the time and interest to make the requested commitment to the volunteer group. Make sure interested members understand the scope of the group—either decision-making or advisory—so they fully grasp the responsibilities or limits to their roles. Solicit input from the group throughout the year through a mix of conference calls and individual contact via phone and email. Try to schedule at least one annual face-to-face meeting. Combining the meeting with the association's annual conference is ideal, as at least a good number of volunteers should be planning to attend. Follow up regularly with group members regarding their specific assignments. For example, an editorial advisory board assignment might be to write a newsletter article or to suggest content ideas and authors for a magazine article.

199. Create a volunteer chart of activities.

Break up activities in time commitments that a member could do if they could volunteer only if they had 5 minutes per week, month, or on a one-time volunteer basis. Do this for several different time increments such as 30 minutes, an hour, and several hours. This will help you place volunteers who want more or less involvement and create more opportunities for people to participate.

SHARE TIPS WITH COLLEAGUES

In our ongoing effort to connect great ideas and great people, we're collecting tips and ideas on a variety of topics that will be reviewed, and *if selected*, will be published in a future publication—a collection of "199" tips on a particular topic. You can choose to be credited as a contributor and if your tip is published be listed in the book as such, or you can choose to remain anonymous. Either way, it's a chance to give back to your profession and help others achieve greater success.

If you have questions about our "199 Ideas" series, please contact the director of book publishing at books@asaecenter.org.

Following is the submission form. We prefer that you visit **www.asaecenter.org/sharemytip** to submit your tip electronically via our website. However, if you prefer, you may copy and submit the form by mail or fax to:

Attn: Director of Book Publishing
ASAE: The Center for Association Leadership
1575 I Street, NW
Washington, DC 20005-1103
Fax: (202) 220-6439

Share My Tip Form

Please select the appropriate category or categories for your tip submission:

Board & Volunteers
- ☐ Board Relations
- ☐ Volunteer Relations
- ☐ Volunteer Recruitment
- ☐ Volunteer Engagement
- ☐ Volunteer Retention/Rewarding

Meetings
- ☐ Sponsorships
- ☐ Connecting Attendees
- ☐ Enhancing Learning Experiences
- ☐ Exhibits
- ☐ Generating Additional Revenue
- ☐ Other: _____

Finance
- ☐ Budgeting
- ☐ Cutting Expenses
- ☐ Other: _____

Benchmarking & Research
- ☐ Increasing Response Rate
- ☐ Other: _____

Membership
- ☐ Recruitment/Retention
- ☐ Communications
- ☐ Engagement
- ☐ Program Benefits
- ☐ Dues Structures
- ☐ Globalization
- ☐ Research
- ☐ Other: _____

Technology
- ☐ Other: _____

Time-Saving Tips
- ☐ Other: _____

Please submit your tip below. Please limit to 500 characters. If you require more than 500 characters, please submit via email directly to books@asaecenter.org with the subject "Tip".

Continued on next page...

Share My Tip Form
continued from previous page

Name: _____

Organization: _____

_____

Email: _____

Please indicate whether you would like to remain anonymous or be credited as a tip contributor if your tip is published:

☐ Anonymous

☐ Yes, please list me as a contributor.

By submitting your tip, you represent and warrant that you are the sole author and proprietor of all rights in the work, that the work is original, that the work has not been previously published, that the work does not infringe any personal or property rights of another, that the work does not contain anything libelous or otherwise illegal, and that you have the authority to enter into this agreement and grant of license. You also agree that the work contains no material from other works protected by copyright that have been used without the written consent of the copyright owner and that ASAE: The Center for Association Leadership is under no obligation to publish your tip submission.

You also grant ASAE: The Center for Association Leadership the following rights: (1) to publish the work in all print, digital, and other known or unknown formats; (2) to reprint, make derivative works of, and otherwise reproduce the work in all print, digital, and other known or unknown formats; and (3) to grant limited sub-licenses to others for the right to reprint, make derivative works of, and otherwise reproduce the work in all print, digital, and other known or unknown formats.

Signature _____

Thank you for submitting your tip!